KT-431-405

C152361422

18

23

KENT ARTS & LIBRARIES	
C152361422	

Pyramid

LONDON, NEW YORK, MUNICH,
MELBOURNE, and DELHI

Written and edited by Caroline Bingham
Designed by Janet Allis

Publishing manager Susan Leonard
Managing art editor Clare Shedden
Jacket design Chris Drew
Picture researchers Sarah Pownall, Jo de Gray
Production Shivani Pandey
DTP Designer Almudena Díaz
Consultant John Malam

First published in Great Britain in 2004 by
Dorling Kindersley Limited
80 Strand, London WC2R 0RL

2 4 6 8 10 9 7 5 3 1

A Penguin Company
Copyright © 2004
Dorling Kindersley Limited, London

A CIP catalogue record for this book
is available from the British Library.

All rights reserved. No part of this publication may be
reproduced, stored in a retrieval system, or transmitted in
any form or by any means, electronic, mechanical,
photocopying, recording, or otherwise, without the prior
written permission of the copyright owner.

ISBN 1-4053-0376-X

Colour reproduction by Colourscan, Singapore
Printed and bound in Italy by L.E.G.O.

see our complete
catalogue at
www.dk.com

Contents

What is a pyramid?

Pyramids are mysterious buildings and many are incredibly old. We know that the world's oldest pyramids, in Egypt, were used as tombs for Egyptian pharaohs, or kings. In other countries, pyramids have been used for religious worship. However, pyramids still hide many secrets.

This sculpture shows the ancient Egyptian pharaoh Menkaure. It gives us a sense of his power and authority.

Nevada, USA
Pyramid Rock

France
Louvre Pyramid

Mexico
Aztec Temple
of Tenochtitlan

Mexico
Chichen Itza

Egypt
Giza pyramids

Sudan
Pyramids at Meroe

India
Brihadisvara Temple

Java
Borobodur Temple

Where are they?
Some countries have hundreds of pyramids, others have none. This map shows the location of some of the major pyramids mentioned in this book.

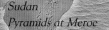

Many Hindu temples have a pyramid shape.

Find a pyramid
A pyramid has four triangular sides that meet at a point. It has a square base. The shape appears in buildings in many parts of the world. Perhaps there is a pyramid near where you live.

Still in use!

The pyramid shape is still used today by architects. This modern 12-storey pyramid in Texas, USA, houses an aquarium. It is built of glass, steel, and concrete: very different materials to the hefty blocks of stone used for the ancient Egyptian pyramids shown below.

Why a pyramid?

Nobody really knows why the pyramid shape was used by the ancient Egyptians. Some believe it is based on the shape of the Sun's rays as they come down to Earth. Others say it was a stairway to heaven. The mystery may never be solved.

The first pyramid

The Step Pyramid at Saqqara, Egypt, is believed to be the world's first pyramid. It was built from small blocks of stone some 4,700 years ago (2,650 BC) and takes its name from its step-like appearance.

Step by step
The Step Pyramid has six levels, or steps, and is a solid structure. It took about 18 years to build.

Djoser's statue was once painted in bright, life-like colours.

The pyramid reaches a height of 60 m (198 ft).

Who was it for?
The Step Pyramid was built for a pharaoh called Djoser. It was built over his burial chamber, which was at the bottom of a 28 m (92 ft) shaft.

A taste for colour
Is your room a bright colour? Even 4,700 years ago, people liked colour. Just look at these blue tiles, found in the Step Pyramid complex.

Walled in

An Egyptian pyramid was often built inside a walled enclosure, and accompanied by other buildings. The site is called a pyramid complex.

This model shows what the Step Pyramid complex once looked like.

The Step Pyramid's enclosure wall was 10.5 m (34 ft) high.

Beneath the complex, Djoser's workers dug out around 5.7 km (2 ½ miles) of tunnels, shafts, and chambers.

Rock of ages

Djoser's burial chamber, cut into the solid rock underneath the Step Pyramid, was lined with red-and-black granite. This building material is still used today.

Who built it?

The architect who built the Step Pyramid, Imhotep, was to become more famous than Djoser. The ancient Egyptians worshipped him more than 2,000 years after his death as a god of wisdom.

Imhotep was Djoser's chief minister, or vizier.

True pyramids

One hundred years after the construction of the Step Pyramid, Egyptian building methods improved dramatically. The pyramids of this period were made up of huge slabs of stone and had straight sides, not steps: the age of the true pyramid had arrived.

Scary surprise

These amazingly lifelike statues of Sneferu's son, Prince Rahotep, and his wife Nofret, were found in a tomb close to the Meidum Pyramid.

The statues scared the workmen who found them because they looked so real.

The Meidum Pyramid was originally a step pyramid. It was later given straight sides. The outer casing has since fallen away to reveal the inner, stepped structure.

Remains of outer casing.

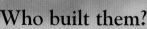

Who built them?

The pharaoh Sneferu built the first straight-sided pyramids. He built three of them. His first was at Meidum. His second is called the Bent Pyramid. His third is the North, or Red, Pyramid.

Bent beginnings

Sneferu's Bent Pyramid started life as a very steep-sided pyramid, but halfway up the builders changed the slope of the sides. This was because the original angle was too steep, and the insides were starting to collapse.

The Bent Pyramid has a large amount of its original outer casing.

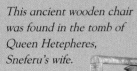

This ancient wooden chair was found in the tomb of Queen Hetepheres, Sneferu's wife.

Third time lucky

Sneferu's builders got it right with their third attempt, the North Pyramid. This is also known as the "Red" Pyramid because of its colour in the sun.

Big and bold

The most famous pyramids of all are those at Giza in Egypt. These three massive tombs were built more than 4,500 years ago and dominate the landscape around them.

Who's who?

The Giza pyramids were built for the pharaohs Khufu, Khafre, and Menkaure. We know what each pharaoh looked liked because archaeologists have found statues of them.

AN AWFUL LOT OF STONE

The French military commander Napoleon Bonaparte estimated that there was enough stone in the three Giza pyramids to build a 3 m (10 ft) high and 0.3 m (1 ft) thick wall around France.

Menkaure's pyramid was the last of the three to be built.

Sun disc

The Egyptians believed the dead pharaoh travelled through the sky in a boat, which also carried the Sun.

These small pyramids are known as the Queen's Pyramids.

The afterlife

The Egyptians believed life continued after death. Pyramids were built to contain the mummified bodies of their kings, the pharaohs. Their mummies were meant to stay in the pyramids for ever, while the pharaohs' spirits travelled to the afterlife.

Khafre's pyramid still has some of its original outer limestone casing.

A bird's eye view

This picture shows how the Giza pyramids may have appeared when first built, with their white limestone outer casings. They would have been enclosed by walls, with flat-topped tombs inside each enclosure.

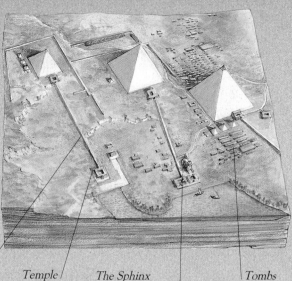

Each pyramid had a causeway, which was a raised path that connected two small temples together.

Temple | The Sphinx sits in front of Khafre's pyramid. | Tombs

Khufu's pyramid, known as the Great Pyramid, is the largest, but appears smaller as it sits on lower ground.

Take a ride

If you visit the Giza pyramids, you may have the chance to ride a camel. You'll certainly see one. Camels have been used in Egypt for well over 2,000 years. They are incredibly well-adapted to the intense and dry heat.

The Great Pyramid

The only known statue of Khufu is just 7.6 cm (3 in) tall.

Visitors to the Great Pyramid are always amazed at its size. At 138 m (450 ft) it is taller than America's Statue of Liberty and covers an area the size of 200 tennis courts. As tall as a 50-storey skyscraper, this is an incredible structure.

All-powerful

The Great Pyramid was built for Khufu. A pharaoh was seen as a living god and people obeyed his commands. Khufu was a powerful pharaoh, but the only statue that remains of him is tiny, and his mummy has been lost.

Which way in?

Hidden under its limestone casing, the pyramid's original entrance was invisible to would-be tomb robbers for thousands of years. Today's visitors use a lower entrance that was created in AD 820 by an Arab leader.

Built for a giant

If you were allowed to climb the Great Pyramid today (it's against the law), you would find it a struggle. Each block is half as tall as an adult – it's a bit like a giant's staircase.

The blocks fit together very tightly.

Up at the top

Today, a wooden tripod on top of the pyramid shows its original height. The Great Pyramid was originally 146 m (479 ft) high, but the peak has worn away over time.

Archaeologists believe that the Great Pyramid originally had a golden cap.

A smooth looker

The Great Pyramid was originally covered in smooth white limestone, which would have shimmered in the sun. More than a tomb, it was a symbol of all the ancient Egyptians believed in. Its creation alone involved thousands of people.

A passing lorry shows the size of the pyramid.

Ancient facts

● All the pyramids had been broken into by 1000 BC.

● The Great Pyramid was the tallest building in the world for 4,300 years, until the Eiffel Tower in Paris, France, was finished in 1889.

● The word pharaoh means "great house".

A look inside

Enter the Great Pyramid today and you will follow
a dimly-lit corridor down until it meets another
that rises quite steeply and opens into the huge
Grand Gallery. Pass on through this and
you will come to the King's Chamber.

Follow that corridor

Inside the Great Pyramid is a network
of shafts and corridors, chambers and
galleries, more complicated than
those of any other pyramid.
Nobody knows for certain just
how they were all used.

*Grand
Gallery*

*King's
Chamber*

*Airshafts leading from the
King's Chamber line up with
certain stars, perhaps to let
the king's soul travel to them.*

*A robot has been used
to explore narrow
shafts leading from the
Queen's Chamber.*

*One of five
relieving chambers.*

*Khufu's burial
chamber contains a
damaged stone sarcophagus.*

Fit for a king

The king's burial chamber lies at the
heart of the pyramid, the weight it
carries supported by five relieving
chambers. The chamber was built
around the king's stone sarcophagus.

The Grand Gallery

After the cramped corridor leading into the pyramid, the fabulously high ceiling of the Grand Gallery comes as a surprise. At 8.5 m (28 ft) tall, a streetlight would fit in here.

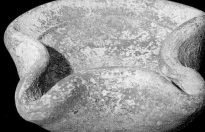

How did they see?

The ancient Egyptians worked on the dark corridors by the flickering light of oil lamps with twisted linen wicks. Over the centuries, the lamps and burning torches of visitors have blackened the polished stone in many areas.

The pyramid's original entrance is on its north side, 15 m (49 ft) above ground level.

The robot towed a computer "brain".

Mystery of the shafts

A robot was recently sent along two of the Great Pyramid's shafts. Pyramid Rover managed to crawl 65 m (208 ft) up a shaft just 20 cm (8 in) across, drill through a tiny door and send back images of a second door.

How was it built?

The Great Pyramid is believed to contain more than two million limestone blocks, each weighing as much as a family-sized car with its passengers. There are 200 layers! All this was built by hand!

How to cut stone

Archaeologists think the blocks were cut by hammering wooden wedges into the rock. The wedges were soaked with water until they expanded and split the rock. The blocks were levered away.

Floating stones

The Great Pyramid was built on the west bank of the River Nile, close to the river, because some stones were taken to the site by boat.

One mighty ramp?

No records exist to tell us exactly how the pyramid was built. One theory is that a ramp was used, increasing in size as each layer was added. Workers dragged the stones up it.

Fine white limestone was used to coat the Great Pyramid.

Archaeologists believe it took around 5,000 workers 23 years to build the Great Pyramid.

It would have been difficult to move stones around the corners.

Winding around?

An alternative theory suggests that the pyramid builders constructed a ramp that spiralled around the pyramid and was later removed.

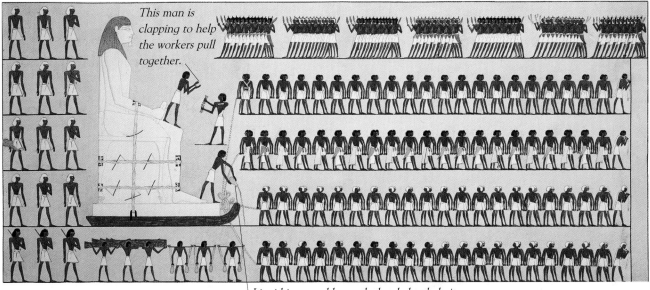

This man is clapping to help the workers pull together.

Liquid is poured beneath the sled to help it move.

A hard pull

The pyramid builders dragged huge loads by hand on wooden sleds. Just look at this picture, taken from a tomb carving made almost 4,000 years ago. It shows 172 men pulling a massive stone statue.

This carpenter is using an adze.

Wooden hammers are still used today.

An adze was used for cutting wood.

The Great Pyramid sits on a solid rock foundation.

Tools of the trade

Archaeologists have found many tools around the pyramid sites, and some of these are very similar to those used today. But the Egyptians only had soft metals to work with.

Building bricks

Later pyramids were built from bricks. Mud from the River Nile was mixed with sand and straw and shaped in wooden moulds. The bricks were then left to dry in the sun.

Who built the pyramids?

The pyramids were built by teams of workers who came to Giza from all over Egypt. They were ordered to do the work for the pharaoh, but they were not slaves. Workers were well-treated. They were given somewhere to live, food and drink, and they had time off to rest.

Fresh from the farm

Many pyramid workers were farmers, who came to help build each year when the Nile flooded their farms and they were unable to work on the land.

Farmland was always on the banks of the Nile.

Grain store

The Egyptians produced some 40 varieties of bread.

How did they live?

A village used by the pyramid workers has been found just 1.6 km (1 mile) from the Great Pyramid. It had shops for bakers, brewers, and butchers, and it had doctors.

Thousands of pots for baking bread have been found near the pyramids.

A meaty diet

Archaeologists have found enough animal bones in the workers' village to feed several thousand people meat every day. Meat was usually reserved for the rich: the pyramid builders were exceptionally well fed.

Huge numbers of cattle, sheep, and goats were cut up and cooked in the workers' village.

This worker is preparing casks of beer.

Bring on the beer

The workers drank plenty of beer, made from barley. It was much thicker than the beer drunk today, like a porridge or gruel.

Barley

Holes once held posts that supported a canopy.

The dormitories would have housed the temporary, or seasonal, workers: the farmers.

And so to bed

In the workers' village, archaeologists have found the remains of what they believe are dormitories, with sleeping space for up to 2,000 people. Some workers had their own small houses.

Untold treasures

Every pyramid was looted long ago, so we can only guess at what treasures might have been buried with Egypt's early pharaohs. Luckily, one pharaoh's tomb was missed by the robbers. He was Tutankhamun and his tomb shows what might have been inside the pyramids.

Talking pictures

We know who was buried in some of the pyramids because of hieroglyphics, a form of writing with pictures. Tombs sometimes included the hieroglyphic name of the pharaoh buried there.

Secret treasure

In 1922 an English archaeologist called Howard Carter made an amazing discovery: the tomb of a young Egyptian pharaoh called Tutankhamun. It was crammed with thousands of treasures.

Tutankhamun's golden throne shows the king with his wife, Ankhesenamun.

Burial mask

Tutankhamun's burial mask is more than 3,000 years old. This incredible piece of work is made from beaten gold, precious glass and stones and weighs about 11 kg (24 lbs).

The boy king

Not much is known about Tutankhamun. He became pharaoh at the age of eight or nine, and died less than ten years later. He may have been murdered by his successor.

Packing for the afterlife

Everything Tutankhamun may have needed in the afterlife was buried with him, including food, jewellery, and furniture. There were even six chariots.

The scarab beetle was often used on Egyptian jewellery. It represented new life.

On guard

Tutankhamun's burial chamber was guarded by two life-size statues. The only reason the tomb had not been robbed long ago was because its entrance had been hidden by the building rubble of a tomb above it.

Brain hook

Ritual knife used for preparing a body for mummification.

Mummy mysteries

A dead pharaoh was not buried straight away. His body was preserved, or mummified, so that his spirit would recognise it in the afterlife. The Egyptians were excellent mummy-makers.

Poking around

Soon after death the brain was drained out through the nose. A knife was then used to make an incision in the left side of the body, ready to remove the organs.

Jars for body organs.

Jars at the ready

After opening the body, the liver, intestines, lungs, and stomach were removed. They were dried, then placed in special jars. These were often topped with heads of different gods.

Get ready with the salt

Next the body was packed with linen or sand, and left under a pile of natron for 40 days. This dried out the body. Finally it was cleaned and wrapped in linen strips.

Natron is a natural salt.

Linen strip

Lucky charms

The cut in the body was covered with a plaque. On it was a sign for the Eye of Horus. It was an amulet, or charm, and was meant to stop evil from entering the body. Many other amulets were placed between the mummy wrappings.

Eye of Horus.

Embalming

The god of mummy-making, Anubis, had the head of a jackal. This picture shows a priest wearing the mask of Anubis making the final preparations over the body of a pharaoh.

Amulets, such as these, were lucky charms. They were believed to offer protection.

The ankh, a symbol of life, was a powerful amulet.

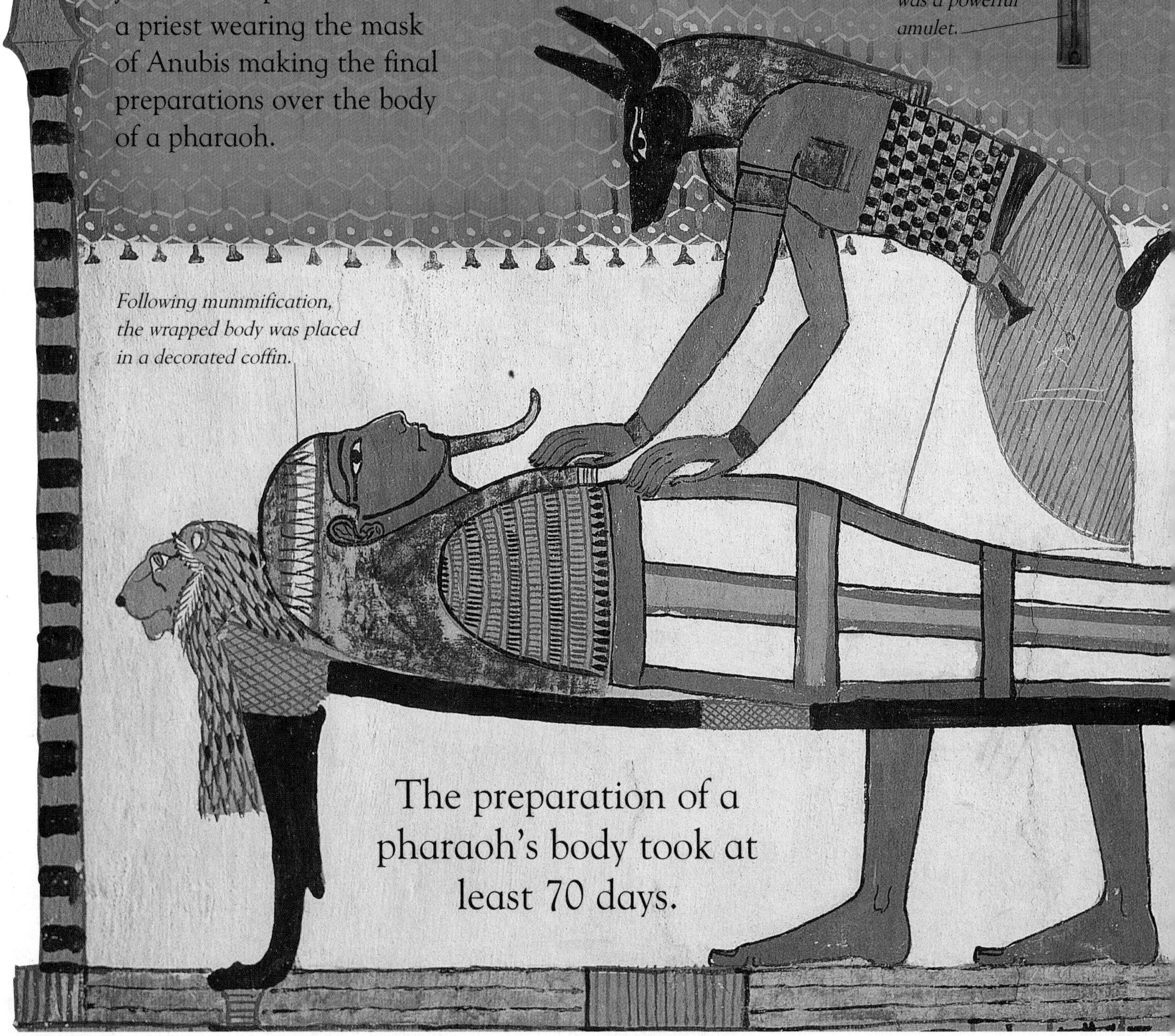

Following mummification, the wrapped body was placed in a decorated coffin.

The preparation of a pharaoh's body took at least 70 days.

23

Mummy revealed

Mummy cases were painted in bright colours and decorated with hieroglyphs.

Lid of outer coffin.

Lid of inner coffin.

In the past, mummies have had some rough treatment. Many were damaged by tomb robbers, while others were ground into powder in the belief it made good medicine. Today, mummies are respected and studied for what they tell us about life in the past.

Mummy cover

Nest of coffins

A wealthy Egyptian might have his or her mummy encased in a "nest" of two or more coffins. A coffin was called a "chest of life". It was another layer of protection for the person's body.

I know that face!

The preservation of a person's face was important to the Egyptians as they believed that a person's spirit had to recognize its body before the mummy could enter the afterlife.

Noses were stuffed with peppercorns and cheeks

The mummy's skeleton can be seen inside its coffin.

Outer coffin

Mummy facts

● The heart was left inside the body. The Egyptians believed it gave a person their intelligence and emotions.

● In the 1800s thousands of mummified cats were brought to England, ground up, and used as fertilizer.

The inside story

Mummies are rarely cut open today. Modern scanning equipment can see through a mummy's coffin and wrappings without damaging either and create a 3D picture of the body inside.

Crocodiles from the River Nile were mummified.

If it moved, mummify it!

The ancient Egyptians also mummified animals – millions of them. Mummified pets were buried with their owners, as were joints of meat to feed the person. Some animal mummies were presents for the gods.

Coffins were made for some animal mummies, such as this one for a shrew.

The Egyptians kept cats as pets, and also mummified them.

with linen wads to keep their shape.

25

Lion or man?

Approach Khafre's pyramid from the east, and prepare to be amazed. This pyramid is guarded by an incredible man-lion, a statue carved out of a lump of rock the size of a jumbo jet. Meet the Sphinx!

A close shave

At some stage in its history, the Sphinx had a beard, but this fell off long ago. This fragment was found in the sand beneath its head.

I've had it up to 'ere

For much of its life, the Sphinx was buried by drifting desert sands – in fact, it was buried up to its neck. It was a good thing, as it has helped to preserve the stone. The Sphinx was fully uncovered in 1925.

As hard as rock?

The Sphinx was carved from soft limestone, but wind and rain have caused a lot of damage to the surface and it has been repaired several times.

The nose was deliberately destroyed in the 1400s by a man called Saim-el-Dahr.

The Sphinx faces east, towards the rising sun.

Is it the pharaoh?

The Sphinx has the body of a lion and, experts believe, a head carved to resemble Khafre himself. Can you spot any similarities between this statue of Khafre and the Sphinx?

Both the Sphinx and Khafre's statue wear a striped headcloth, a nemes, which is a symbol of ancient Egyptian royalty.

A MESSAGE IN A DREAM

A tablet between the Sphinx's front paws tells of Thutmosis IV who, in around 1400 BC, fell asleep beneath the Sphinx and dreamt that he would be made a king should he clear away the sand that was burying the Sphinx. Thutmosis did this – and he became king. The sands later returned.

A watery highway

The ancient Egyptians used the River Nile as their major "road". Boats travelled up and down it all the time, including the funeral boats that transported the mummified pharaohs to their pyramids and other tombs.

Row, row, row your boat

Paintings like this show us what Egyptian river boats looked like. These are big boats, which are rowed through the water. Men at the back operate the long steering oars.

Papyrus reed

Reed on

The best boats were made of wood, but most Egyptian boats were made of papyrus reeds, which grew on the banks of the Nile. These were lashed together in a similar way to reed boats used in Peru today.

No rudder

Ancient Egyptian boats were steered with long steering oars – there were no rudders. This model boat is carrying a mummy. Model boats were often buried with the mummy.

The steering oars were at the back, or stern, of the boat.

Sealed in a pit

In 1954, an archaeologist found two boat pits by the Great Pyramid. One contained 1,224 pieces of timber, which joined together to make a boat. This may have carried Khufu's mummy to his pyramid.

No nails here

Khufu's boat is held together with wooden pegs and rope. No metal nails were used because they didn't exist. It was chiselled from blocks of wood.

Tests revealed that Khufu's boat had been used.

A trip to the Sudan

The Sudan lies south of Egypt, in north-east Africa. It is big. In fact, it is just over one-quarter the size of America. About 180 small pyramids have been found here. These steep-sided pyramids were built as royal tombs.

Each pyramid has a small chapel on its eastern side.

A place for offerings

The Sudanese pyramids were built from around 720 BC to AD 350. They all face the rising sun and each has a small chapel in which pilgrims and priests would say prayers for the dead king and queen, and leave offerings for them.

This is one of King Taharqa's shabtis. He is the most famous of the kings buried in the Sudan.

Each shabti had the name of the king with whom it was buried.

This shabti holds farming tools.

Added protection

The kings and queens buried beneath these pyramids were accompanied by shabtis. These small figures were servants whose duty was to serve the king in the next life.

This gold bracelet is decorated with images of a goddess called Mut. Queen Amanishakhto would have worn several bracelets at once.

Tests have shown that the jewellery found in Amanishakhto's tomb had been worn, probably by the Queen herself.

Treasure, too?

Queen Amanishakhto's pyramid at Meroe, in the Sudan, is remarkable as it is the only pyramid of all those in the Sudan and Egypt that has been found with its treasure. The Queen lived in the 1st century BC.

Most pyramids have been damaged, some by treasure hunters looking for valuables.

Some pyramids have been restored.

All for greed

Queen Amanishakhto's treasure was discovered in 1830 by an Italian adventurer called Giuseppe Ferlini. He said he found it at the top of her pyramid. This led others to knock the tops off these little pyramids in a greedy search for treasure.

A trip to Java

Two and a half thousand years ago a teacher called the Buddha set up a religion we call Buddhism. Central to Buddhism is the temple, and one of the oldest of these is the pyramid-shaped Borobodur Temple, in Java, Indonesia.

Borobodur facts

● The word Borobodur means "temple on the hill".

● It is believed that Borobodur took more than 100 years to build.

● The winding walk from bottom to top, properly done, covers almost 5 km (3 miles).

A stepped pyramid

Borobodur is thought to have been built about 1,200 years ago. It looks a little like a stepped pyramid and contains statues of the Buddha on each of its levels, most enclosed in a bell-shaped shrine, or stupa.

Hard times

Soon after it was built, Borobodur was abandoned after an earthquake and it fell into ruin. It was rediscovered in 1814 and has been gradually rebuilt.

Each stupa is pierced with diamond-shaped holes.

Take a left

People work their way up by always turning to the left, and keeping the structure to their right. On the way they pass numerous Buddha statues. There are also carved scenes that tell stories about the life of the Buddha.

Three circular terraces at the top lead to a large central stupa.

The top cannot be seen from the bottom.

A trip to India

Imagine hauling 16 elephants to the top of this pyramid-shaped temple. That's about the weight of the granite dome that tops the Brihadisvara Temple in southern India. How did the builders do it? They used a ramp.

The dome was dragged up an earth ramp that stretched more than 6 km (4 m).

A place of worship

The Brihadisvara (or "Big") Temple was built about 1,000 years ago and has been in continuous use ever since. It stands 63 m (216 ft) high and has 13 floors. Only Hindus are allowed to enter.

Who built it?

Brihadisvara was built by a Chola king. The Cholas ruled much of Southern India from the 800s to the 1200s. They left behind many beautiful buildings, and also a huge number of bronze statues.

On guard

The gates around the Big Temple are decorated with amazingly detailed carvings. The Cholas believed that these sculptures helped to turn away evil spirits.

The sculptures of gods, goddesses, demons, and other creatures are painted in bright colours.

Decorate that pyramid

The pyramid shape can also be seen in many south Indian temple gateways. This gateway is adorned with more than 1500 sculptures. The temple, the Meenakshi, was begun in the 1400s.

Hindu stone carver

The stone carvings seen on Indian temples were carved by hand, a craft that takes great skill. Stonemasons still carve statues like them in parts of India.

A mason will work on a sculpture for several weeks.

Built for sacrifice

The Mayans were a people who lived in Mexico and parts of Central America hundreds of years ago. They built pyramid-shaped temples to use for sacrifice, killing people to keep their gods happy. One of these temples is El Castillo at Chichen Itza.

The Mayans

If you had met a Mayan priest some 1700 years ago, you would have noticed his high, sloping forehead. The Mayans achieved this by strapping a baby's head between two wooden boards to force the skull to grow in a certain way.

Carved stone heads show us how the Mayans may have looked.

Serpent guards

The Mayan name for El Castillo is Kukulkan, the plumed serpent God. Twice a year the sun's position causes a shadow that looks like a snake to run down its side. Two carved snake heads flank the foot of the north staircase.

El Castillo's four stairways each have 91 steps. The step to the platform at the top makes a total of 365 steps.

I'd just like to say...

El Castillo rises steeply to a height of 24 m (78 ft) and gives its visitors a stunning view. It is said that if you stand at the top and speak in a normal voice, you can be heard at the bottom.

Offerings were placed on the chac mool's plate.

Ready and waiting

A statue called a chac mool has usually been found in Mayan temples. The Mayan priests supplied it with incense... or gave it the hearts of their victims.

A little bit of colour

Every evening a sound and light show brings a little bit of colour to El Castillo. The Mayans used a lot of colour in decorative murals, and the temple may well have been brightly painted with murals and signs.

Jungle ruins

Deep in the rainforests of Mexico and Central America are thousands of ruined pyramids, built by the different peoples who lived in this region hundreds of years ago. Some have been restored.

Lord Pacal died in AD 683.

A face from the past

This mosaic burial mask was found in the burial chamber of a Mayan lord called Pacal. He ruled over the city of Palenque, shown below, more than 1,300 years ago.

Most Mayan pyramids were built between AD 600 and 900.

There are said to be 500 buildings in the rainforest at

Mayan pyramids have steep stairs and flat tops with temple chambers.

Hidden riches

The ancient Mexican city of Palenque is hidden in thick rainforest. Deep within Palenque's pyramid temple is Lord Pacal's burial chamber. It contained many beautiful jade objects.

The steps are so steep that the priests zig-zagged up and down them.

An ancient calender

The Mayan Pyramid of the Niches at El Tajín in Mexico contains three hundred and sixty-five niches. According to legend, each niche contained an idol for each day of the year. It is thought to date to AD 600.

Palenque awaiting excavation.

Mayan incense burner from Tikal

Filled with rubble

Another Mayan pyramid is at Tikal in Guatemala (in Central America). Unlike the Egyptian pyramids, Mayan pyramids are not made from solid blocks but have a stone casing laid over rubble.

The Aztecs

The Aztecs were a war-like people who lived in Mexico some 700 years ago. They believed in sacrificing human victims to please their gods, and built pyramid-shaped temples on which to carry this out.

The importance of gods

The Aztecs worshipped many gods, each linked to a particular part of nature. This vase carries an image of Tlaloc, the god of rain.

This painted terracotta vase dates to between 1440 and 1469.

A warrior nation

Aztec warriors were rewarded with fancy costumes for their bravery in war and for the numbers of victims they captured. The more feathers in his headdress, the braver the warrior.

Sacrificial knife

Knives for sacrifice were made from a stone called obsidian or from flint. They were often decorated, sometimes with fierce faces.

A story in pictures

This stone tells of the Aztec belief that the universe had passed through four creations and entered the fifth. All would end violently unless the gods were calmed with human blood. Hence the need for sacrifice.

The stone measures 4 m (13 ft) across!

Two shrines topped the Great Temple. One was dedicated to the god of rain, the other to the god of war.

The Great Temple was just one-fifth the height of Egypt's Great Pyramid.

Mine is the biggest!

The Aztec pyramids were destroyed in the 1600s. This is a model of the Great Temple of Tenochtitlan, Mexico City. It shows how ruler after ruler built ever bigger temples over the original.

Skull mask

More than 6,000 objects were found at the site of the Great Temple, including this human skull mask. Shell and stone "eyes" give it a gruesome appearance.

Weird and wonderful

Some people believe that pyramids have strange and mystical powers. There is even a theory that the Giza pyramids are spaceships, and carried creatures to Earth from other planets. The pyramid shape fascinates people, and is used in lots of different ways today.

A topsy-turvy world

This unusual, upside-down pyramid is actually a shopping centre in Florida, USA. It also contains an aquarium.

Weird facts

- In the 1400s, some people thought the Giza pyramids had been built to store grain in times of famine.

- There's an odd idea that a blunt razor blade will magically sharpen if left in the centre of a model pyramid.

Pyramid lake

Pyramid Lake in Nevada, USA, is aptly named. It has a natural pyramid formation, built up out of a soft rock called tufa. The lake is big and popular with fishermen.

Let's slide down a pyramid

This pyramid was built in the shape of a Mayan Temple, in a waterpark in the Bahamas. It contains five waterslides. The steepest slide carries its riders through a clear tunnel under a shark-infested pool!

The gardens were packed with exotic plants.

The hanging gardens

Nobody knows what the fabled Hanging Gardens of Babylon really looked like, but many modern drawings show them as being set on a pyramid-shaped base.

These luscious gardens existed some 2,600 years ago.

Modern pyramids

Pyramids are still being built today. Modern pyramids show how dramatically building techniques, and materials, have changed.

Short and squat

Pyramids come in all shapes and sizes. This pyramid's broad base supports a fairly low-level building, which is used as an office housing some 675 people. Its reflection in the water provides a dramatic look.

The Louvre

This glass and steel pyramid was built as the new entrance to the Louvre Museum in Paris, in 1989. A lot of people hated it at first, but it is now a popular feature of the Museum.

Spend a night in a pyramid

Is it real or is it make-believe? This Great Pyramid lookalike is actually a huge hotel in Las Vegas in America. The sphinx that sits outside is larger than the one in Egypt. Its eyes shoot beams of laser light.

The pyramid contains more than 2,000 rooms.

Built to last

This American pyramid, built as an office block in San Francisco, was designed to withstand the effects of an earthquake. It is much taller than Giza's Great Pyramid, but its base is tiny in comparison. One-fifth of its height is taken up by its spire.

The spire is coated in aluminium, a lightweight metal.

The pyramid is 260 m (853 ft) tall.

Glossary

Here are the meanings of some words it is useful to know
when learning about pyramids.

AD the letters stand for Anno Domini, meaning 'in the year of our Lord' and are placed before the date, starting with AD 1.

adze a tool used to cut and smooth wood.

amulet a lucky charm.

ancient Egypt the time that Egypt was ruled by pharaohs. It lasted from around 3100 BC to 30 BC.

archaeologist a person who studies the remains of past human life and activities.

Aztec a Central American civilization that was based largely in Mexico. The Aztec culture crumbled under Spanish invaders in the 1500s.

BC the letters stand for 'Before Christ' and are placed after the date, ending with 1 BC.

Eye of Horus an ancient Egyptian sign that symbolized healing, strength, and perfection.

god a being or number of beings worshipped by people. Ancient Egyptian gods and goddesses took many different forms, both human and animal.

granite a hard-wearing stone that was used by the ancient Egyptians for sculpture, stone coffins, and for lining the inside of some tombs and chambers.

hieroglyphs ancient Egyptian picture writing. Ancient Egyptian scribes used at least 700 different picture symbols.

Imhotep Djoser's chief minister, or vizier. He designed the Step Pyramid, Egypt's first pyramid. He was worshipped 2,000 years after his death. Bronze statues usually depict him as a learned scholar with a papyrus roll.

Mayans a Central American people with an advanced civilization, whose way of life collapsed during the 800s.

metal the ancient Egyptians did not have many metals. They used bronze, copper, and gold, all of which are fairly soft.

mummification the process of preserving a dead body from decay.

mummy a preserved body, either human or animal.

natron a natural salt that is still used today in baking soda.

nemes a pleated linen headcloth worn by ancient Egyptian pharaohs, denoting their royal status.

niche a shallow recess in a wall. It is usually used to display a statue.

papyrus a riverside reed used by the ancient Egyptians to make all sorts of things, including a form of paper, sandals, baskets, and rope.

pharaoh an ancient Egyptian king or queen.

pyramidion a pyramid-shaped stone that capped the top of a pyramid.

sacrifice the killing of a person or animal as part of a religious ceremony.

sarcophagus an outer coffin made of stone.

shabti small human figures that were believed to work for the person they were buried with in the afterlife.

sphinx a statue that has the body of a lion and the face of a person.

temple a building used for religious worship.

tomb a grave or building where a dead person is placed.

vizier the highest official in the ancient Egyptian government. The vizier reported directly to the pharaoh.

Index

Acknowledgements

Dorling Kindersley would like to thank:
Thanks to Janet Allis for original artwork, and to Sarah Mills and Kate Ledwith for DK Picture Library research.

Picture credits

The publisher would like to thank the following for their kind permission to reproduce their photographs:
Key: a=above; c=centre; b=below; l=left; r=right; t=top

Alamy Images: Claudia Adams 12c; Bygonetimes 21br; Robert Harding Picture Library 28-29; M. Joecks 39cr; Ian McKinnell 9cr; John Ross/Robert Harding Picture Library 15tc; Worldthroughthelens 20br. **Todd N. Alexander:** 13tr. **Ancient Art & Architecture Collection:** 15tr, 25cl; J. Stevens 14cl. **The Art Archive:** Egyptian Museum Cairo/Dagli Orti 12tl; Museo Regional de Antropologia Merida Mexico/Dagli Orti 37tr; Museo del Tempo Mayor Mexico/Dagli Orti 40ca; Staatliche Sammlung Agyptischer Kunst Munich/Dagli Orti 31tl. **Art Directors & TRIP:** A. Tovy 17br, 18c. **Bildarchiv Preußischer Kulturbesitz:** 31tr. Bridgeman Art Library, London/New York: British Museum, London, UK 36tl. **Corbis:** 10-11, 26-27; Lynsey Addario 40-41; Archivo Iconografico, S.A 6tl, 8c, 10bl, 18tr, 23b, 36bl; David Cumming; Eye Ubiquitous 35c; Macduff Everton 39bc, 43tr; Mark E. Gibson 5tr; Richard Hamilton Smith 44tr; Rose Hartman 42-43; Lindsay Hebberd 35tl, 35bc; Robert Holmes 4bl, 44-45; Hulton-Deutsch Collection 26cl; Richard Klune 45tr; Danny Lehman 38-39, 39tl; Charles & Josette Lenars 39tr; Chris Lisle 35tr; Landmann Patrick/Sygma 24-25b; Carmen Redondo 29br; Bill Ross 37br; Scott T. Smith 4cla, 43tl; Hubert Stadler 28bl; Stapleton Collection 20cl; Orban Thierry/Sygma 33tr; Vanni Archive 29cla; Sandro Vannini 8tl; Roger Wood 4tl, 12bl, 21tr, 27tr; Michael S. Yamashita 4cr, 4cb, 30-31, 34-35. **DK Images:** Bolton Metro Museum 16-17b; British Museum 2tc, 6bc, 7br, 17cra, 17crb, 17t, 18bl, 19cl, 22tl, 22cra, 22bc, 22br, 23cra, 24tl, 25cr, 25cbr, 26tc, 29tr, 30bl, 48c; INAH 3, 4cbl, 41tc, 41br; The Manchester Museum, The University of Manchester 23car; Rosicrucian Egyptian Museum, San Jose, California 7t. **Werner Forman Archive:** 19tr, 32bl; Egyptian Museum, Cairo 9c, 16cla, 21c, 23tr, 28cl; Teresa McCullough Collection, London 34cl; National Museum of Anthropology, Mexico City 38tl, 41tr; Staatlich Museum, Berlin 17c; E. Strouhal 18bc. **Getty Images:** AFP 19bl, 30cl; Guildo Alberto Rossi 5; Richard A Cooke III 36-37; Grant Faint 40l; Will & Deni McIntyre 13. **Robert Harding Picture Library:** Advertasia 4crb; Tettoni Casio 32-33; I.Vanderharst 1. **Masterfile UK:** Miles Ertman 20-21c. **Peabody Museum, Harvard University:** Photo by Jim Harrison 18br. **Reuters:** Aladin Abdel Naby 15br. **Science Photo Library:** Brian Brake 20l; Christian Jegou, Publiphoto Diffusion 22cl; Alexander Tsiaras 25tc.

All other images © Dorling Kindersley www.dkimages.com